_____

*To*

_____

*From*

Our days are so crowded and our hours are so few,

And there's so little time and so much to do,

That the days fly by and are over and done

Before we have even half begun

To do the things that we meant to do

But never have time to carry through—

And how nice it would be if we stopped to say

The things we feel in our hearts each day!

# The Helen Steiner Rice Foundation

When someone does a kindness

it always seems to me

That's the way God up in heaven

would like us all to be . . .

Whatever the celebration, whatever the day, whatever the event, whatever the occasion, Helen Steiner Rice possessed the ability to express the appropriate feeling for that particular moment. A happening became happier, a sentiment more sentimental, a memory more memorable because of her deep sensitivity and ability to put into understandable language the emotion being experienced. Her positive attitude, her concern for others, and her love of God are identifiable threads woven into her life, her work . . . and even her death.

Prior to Mrs. Rice's passing, she established the Helen Steiner Rice Foundation, a nonprofit corporation that awards grants to worthy charitable programs assisting the elderly and the needy. Royalties from the sale of this book will add to the financial capabilities of the Helen Steiner Rice Foundation. Because of limited resources, the foundation presently limits grants to qualified charitable programs in Lorain, Ohio, where Helen Steiner Rice was born, and Greater Cincinnati, Ohio, where Mrs. Rice lived and worked most of her life. Hopefully in the future, resources will be of sufficient size that broader geographical areas may be considered in the awarding of grants.

Because of her foresight, caring, and deep conviction of sharing, Helen Steiner Rice continues to touch a countless number of lives through foundation grants and through her inspirational poetry. Thank you for your assistance in helping to keep Helen's dream alive and growing.

*Andrea E. Cornett,*
**ADMINISTRATOR**

# MOTHER,
## I Love You

### HELEN STEINER RICE
### AND
### VIRGINIA J. RUEHLMANN

Fleming H. Revell
A Division of Baker Book House
Grand Rapids, Michigan 49516

Published by Fleming H. Revell
a division of Baker Book House Company
P.O. Box 6287, Grand Rapids, MI 49516-6287

Second printing, January 2002

Printed in the United States of America

**Library of Congress Cataloging-in-Publication Data**

Rice, Helen Steiner.
      Mother, I love you / Helen Steiner Rice and Virginia  J.
Ruehlmann.
            p.   cm.
      ISBN 0-8007-1764-3 (cloth)
      1. Mothers—Poetry. 2. Motherhood—Poetry. 3.  Mother and child—
Poetry. 4.  Christian poetry, American. I.  Ruehlmann, Virginia  J.
II.  Title.
      PS3568.I28M66   1999
      811'.54—dc21                                                             98-41203

Jacket and interior paintings by Jim Daly

# Contents

To
MY MOTHER,

*Florence Doogan Juergens,*

AND

MY MOTHER-IN-LAW,

*Hattie Mehrckens Ruehlmann*

# Introduction

In all the world there is no relationship as enduring as that which exists between mother and child. A mother's love begins with the divine mystery of the creation of human life and continues as she offers prayers to keep her offspring on "the road less traveled."

Helen Steiner Rice had a genuine appreciation for all mothers and composed many poems celebrating motherhood. As you read and enjoy this book, treasure the memories of days gone by and look forward to the memories yet to be made.

*Virginia J. Ruehlmann*

Mother

# A Mother's Love

Whether she's here or in heaven,

    Mother's love is our haven and guide,

For always the memory of Mother

    is a beacon light shining inside.

Time cannot destroy the memory,

    and years can never erase

The tenderness and the beauty

    of the love in a mother's face.

And when we think of our mothers,

    we draw nearer to God above,

For only God in His greatness

    could fashion a mother's love.

*Her children rise up and call her blessed; her husband also, and he praises her: "Many women have done excellently, but you surpass them all."*

**PROVERBS 31:28–29**

*This painting takes place around the turn of the century. A new citizen is about to be born—the first of this family to be born in the new country.*

Jim Daly

# Mother Is Expecting

Nothing can compare to the sweet excitement of learning that a baby is on the way. Anticipation, joy, and much prayer combine to create a thrilling and wonderful experience.

*For stitching a quilt, crocheting and knitting booties, caps, and mittens,*
*for taking care of your health and the health of family members,*
*for lovingly and carefully preparing for the new arrival,*

## Mother, I love you!

VJR

*The sweetest thing
in all the world is
a mother's love.*

**O. A. NEWLIN**

# Motherhood

The dearest gifts that heaven holds,
 the very finest too,
Were made into one pattern
 that was perfect, sweet, and true.
The angels smiled, well pleased, and said,
 "Compared to all the others,
This pattern is so wonderful,
 let's use it just for mothers!"
And through the years a mother has been
 all that's sweet and good,
For there's a bit of God and love
 in all true motherhood.

A baby is a gift of life
　　　　born of the wonder of love—
A little bit of eternity
　　　　sent from the Father above,
Giving a new dimension
　　　　to the love between husband and wife
And putting an added new meaning
　　　　to the wonder and mystery of life.

# What Is a Baby?

*Lo, sons are a heritage from the LORD,*
*the fruit of the womb a reward.*

**PSALM 127:3**

# Mother Is a Word Called *Love*

Mother is a word called love,

And all the world is mindful of

That the love that's given and shown to others

Is different from the love of mothers.

For mothers play the leading roles

In giving birth to little souls—

For though small souls are heaven sent

And we realize they're only lent,

It takes a mother's loving hands

And her gentle heart that understands

To mold and shape this little life

And shelter it from storm and strife.

No other love than mother love
Could do the things required of
The one to whom God gives the keeping
Of His wee lambs, awake or sleeping.
So mothers are a special race
God sent to earth to take His place,
And "mother" is a lovely name
That even saints are proud to claim.

*Mother love is the fuel that enables a normal human being to do the impossible.*

**AUTHOR UNKNOWN**

15

# LIFE'S FAIREST

I have a garden within my soul
     of wondrous beauty rare
Wherein the blossoms of all my life
     bloom ever in splendor fair.
The fragrance and charm of that garden
     where all of life's flowers bloom
Fill my aching heart with sweet content
     and banish failure's gloom.
Each flower a message is bringing,
     a memory of someone dear,
A picture of deepest devotion
     dispelling all doubt and fear.

# FLOWER

Amid all this beauty and splendor,
     one flower stands forth as queen—
For never a flower existed
     like the blossom I can claim.
For after years I now can see
     amid life's roses and rue
God's greatest gift to a little child,
     my darling mother, was you.

*Charm is deceitful, and beauty is vain, but a woman who fears the LORD is to be praised. Give her of the fruit of her hands, and let her works praise her in the gates.*

**PROVERBS 31:30–31**

# Mother
## and Baby

The telephone spreads the news! Baby has arrived. Mother and new-born are doing fine—and Father too! Is the baby a boy? a girl? What name did you choose? How much does the baby weigh? When can we see Mom and the new addition? We want to welcome the newest member of our family.

*For making our home a place of warmth, love, and security,*
*for radiating devotion, tenderness, and commitment to your family,*
*for emphasizing the importance of each family member,*

## Mother, I love you!

VJR

# WELCOME,

Welcome, dear baby, to a world that is new—

You've been eagerly awaited by your mom, and Dad too.

You're starting life surrounded by love on every side,

And your mom and dad behold you with pleasure and with pride.

You've embarked on a venture that is very strange and new,

And you have to get acquainted with the world surrounding you.

But with such great parents to introduce you, dear,

You'll soon get used to living happily down here.

You will have a lot of sunny days and many happy hours,

But remember with the sunshine there will always be some showers.

# Dear Baby

For life must be a mixture both of sunshine and of rain,

Of joy and of sorrow, mixed with pleasure and with pain,

But God will always be there to help and bless you too,

As you grow into adulthood and all your dreams come true.

And in everything you do, remember to be kind,

And may you look at people with your heart, not just your mind.

For remember our Creator looks down from heaven above,

So live always in His likeness and learn to share His love.

So welcome, dear baby, to this world strange and new,

And God bless your family, who are all in love with you.

# Congratulations

We're happy for you both
　　because your precious baby's birth
Is sure to make your happy home
　　a bit of heaven on earth,
For there's nothing like a baby,
　　so cuddly, small, and sweet,
To give live added meaning
　　and to make it more complete.
And, of course, we're mighty selfish
　　in our happiness for you

Because you see, dear children,
　　you've made us happy too,
For there's nothing like a grandchild
　　to boast of and adore
And to bring back precious memories
　　of your babyhood once more.
And with our loving wishes
　　comes a deep and heartfelt prayer—
God keep you and your baby
　　safely in His daily care.

A wee bit of heaven
  drifted down from above—
A handful of happiness,
  a heart full of love.
The mystery of life
  so sacred and sweet,
The giver of joy
  so deep and complete.
Precious and priceless,
  so lovable too—
The world's sweetest miracle,
  baby, is you.

# Baby

*Babies are bits of stardust blown from the hand of God. Lucky the woman who knows the pangs of birth, for she has held a star.*

**LARRY BARRETO**

Jim Daly
© 1990

# Mother and Child

Days have a way of turning into weeks, weeks into months, and months into years. All the time, love intensifies. Mother, your caring, preparing, serving, and sharing made our house a home.

*For teaching and explaining right from wrong,*
*for lovingly bathing, feeding, and rocking each child,*
*for being a living sermon and a bright and shining light,*
*for adding laughter, music, and tenderness to my life each day,*

## Mother, I love you!

VJR

# A Child's Faith

"Jesus loves me, this I know,

For the Bible tells me so . . ."

Little children ask no more,

For love is all they're looking for,

And in a small child's shining eyes

The faith of all the ages lies.

And tiny hands and tousled heads

That kneel in prayer by little beds

Are closer to the dear Lord's heart

And of His kingdom more a part

Than we who search and never find

The answers to our questioning minds—

For faith in things we cannot see

Requires a child's simplicity.

*I shall never forget my mother, for it was she who planted and nurtured the first seeds of good within me.*

**IMMANUEL KANT**

God made the sun,

   He made the sky,

He made the trees

   and the birds that fly.

God made the flowers,

   He made the light,

He made the stars

   that shine at night.

*Beauty is God's
handwriting.*

**CHARLES KINGSLEY**

# God's Handiwork

God made the rain,

   He made the dew,

And He made

   loving mothers too—

Dear and special

   ones like you!

# In the Storms of *Life*

A mother's love is like an island

    in life's ocean vast and wide—

A peaceful, quiet shelter

    from the restless, rising tide.

A mother's love is like a fortress,

    and we seek protection there,

When the waves of tribulation

    seem to drown us in despair.

A mother's love's a sanctuary

    where our souls can find sweet rest

From the struggle and the tension

    of life's fast and futile quest.

A mother's love is like a tower
　　　　rising far above the crowd,
And her smile is like the sunshine
　　　　breaking through a threatening cloud.
A mother's love is like a beacon
　　　　burning bright with faith and prayer,
And through the changing scenes of life
　　　　we find a haven there.
For a mother's love is fashioned
　　　　after God's unfailing love—
It is endless and unfailing
　　　　like the love of Him above.

*A mother's arms are made of tenderness and children sleep soundly in them.*

**VICTOR HUGO**

# A Great Career Is Motherhood

So glad a tiny baby came
To share your life and love and name,
For no doubt she is the greatest claim
That you have ever had to fame.
And don't misunderstand me, dear,
You were a star in your career,
But what, I ask you, is success
Compared with heaven's happiness?

And how could plaudits anywhere
Be half as wonderful and fair?
For this experience of the heart
Surpasses any skill or art,
For man excels in every line
But woman has a gift divine,
And in this world there is no other
As greatly honored as a mother.

*Happiness comes of the capacity to feel deeply, to enjoy simply, to think freely, to risk life, to be needed.*

**STORM JAMESON**

# UNENDING *Love*

Only through the years
    of patience and sharing
Do you earn the priceless
    and rich joy of caring.
And memories are treasures
    time cannot destroy—
They're made of pure gold
    without any alloy.
And those happy years
    so devotedly spent
Bring you a harvest
    of peace and content,
For life and its problems
    are only a blending
Of a love that's divine
    and also unending.

*"Make-believe"*
*was a part of*
*growing up for*
*all of us and, in*
*a way, is still a*
*part of adult*
*life. The baby*
*buggy in this*
*painting is from*
*the past; it con-*
*tinues to be cher-*
*ished by a child*
*making-believe,*
*just as it was by*
*her mother and*
*grandmother*
*before her.*

Jim Daly

Jim Daly
©
1987

# Mother's Love

"Nothing to do? Use your imagination," you often said. "Pretend you are a mother. Does your doll need changing? Is she hungry? You can show your love in many small ways." There are so many chores for a mother to do. Mothers do them with love, and they don't seem to mind at all.

*For teaching me life's lessons in many ways,*
*for encouraging delight in inexpensive but enjoyable activities,*
*for sharing an appreciation of nature and other gifts from God,*

## Mother, I love you!

VJR

# The Little
## *Heartbreakers*

Who steals into your heart

with magical touch?

Who ensnares your love

in a wee angel clutch?

Who makes you a slave

and a worshiper too?

Who gets adoration

so lavish and true?

Who plays with your heartstrings

like champion love makers?

Nobody but babies—

the little heartbreakers.

*Children are the most wholesome part of the race and the sweetest for they are the freshest from the hand of God.*

**HERBERT HOOVER**

*Memories*

Tender little memories
    of some word or deed
Give us strength and courage
    when we are in need.
Blessed little memories
    help to bear the cross
And soften all the bitterness
    of failure and of loss.
Precious little memories
    of little things we've done
Make the very darkest day
    a bright and happy one.

*Train a child in the way he
should go, and when he is
old he will not turn from it.*

**PROVERBS 22:6 NIV**

# Hush~a~Bye

Hush-a-bye, hush-a-bye, my sleepyhead—
Angels are waiting to tuck you in bed.
Go to sleep, go to sleep, close your bright eyes—
Nighttime is tumbling out of the skies.
Angels are waiting, their vigil to keep—
The sandman is filling your wee eyes with sleep.
Hush-a-bye, hush-a-bye, my little sweet—
Playtime is over for tired, tiny feet.
Close your eyes, honey, sleepytime's here—
Good night, little darling, good night, little dear.

# Where Does the Time Go?

Where does the time go in its endless flight?

Spring turns to fall and day turns to night,

And little girls grow up and marry,

For years fly by and do not tarry,

And though it seems like yesterday

That she was busily at play,

The months and years have quickly flown

And your small doll is now full grown,

And instead of pinafores and curls,

She's joined the ranks of married girls.

I simply can't believe it's true,

And I know it's hard for you parents too,

To realize your baby's grown

And from the nest your "little bird" has flown.

# THE HEART OF THE *Home*

Memories to treasure
     are made every day—
Made of family gatherings
     and children as they play—
And always it is Mother
     who plays the leading part
In bringing joy and happiness
     to each expectant heart.
For no one gives more happiness
     or does more good for others
Than understanding, kind, and wise,
     and selfless, loving mothers.
And of all the loving mothers,
     the dearest one is you,
For you live your faith every day
     in everything you do.

*The mother's heart is the child's schoolroom.*

**HENRY WARD BEECHER**

# A Mother's Love

A mother's love is something
that no one can explain—
It is made of deep devotion
and of sacrifice and pain.
It is endless and unselfish
and enduring, come what may,
For nothing can destroy it
or take that love away.
It is patient and forgiving
when all others are forsaking,
And it never fails or falters
even though the heart is breaking.

It believes beyond believing
when the world around condemns,
And it glows with all the beauty
of the rarest, brightest gems.
It is far beyond defining,
it defies all explanation,
And it still remains a secret
like the mysteries of creation—
A many-splendored miracle
we cannot understand,
And another wondrous evidence
of God's tender, guiding hand.

*Getting a haircut, or getting your ears lowered as we used to call it, usually meant going to the barber shop; but when times were hard or you lived too far out in the country, a pair of scissors and a skilled mom or dad would do the job.*

Jim Daly

© Jim Daly 1980

# Mother's Encouragement

Snip, snip here—brush and comb there. The lesson was "Take pride
in yourself and always look and act your best."

*For encouraging me to be the best I could be,*

*for developing the potential within each family member,*

*for training me to see the value and worth of each individual,*

*for teaching me that a happy, positive attitude and a smile are more*

*valuable than an expensive wardrobe,*

## Mother, I love you!

VJR

# Mothers Are Special

Mothers are special people
    in a million different ways
And merit loving compliments
    and many words of praise.
For a mother's aspiration
    is for her family's success,
To make the family proud of her
    and bring them happiness.

*My mother was the most
beautiful woman I ever saw.
All I am I owe to my mother.
I attribute all my success in
life to the moral, intellectual,
and physical education I
received from her.*

**GEORGE WASHINGTON**

# Your Son

When your son was just a little boy,
You always found your greatest joy
In watching him from day to day
Exploring new worlds in his play.
For with a kite string in his hand
He soared into an unknown land,
And with uplifted childish eyes,
He tried to penetrate the skies.
For little hands and minds reach out
To learn what life is all about,
And God in wisdom and in love
Directs His children's eyes above.

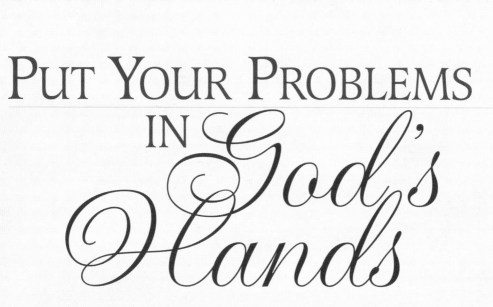

# PUT YOUR PROBLEMS IN *God's Hands*

Although it sometimes seems to us
    our prayers have not been heard,
God always knows our every need
    without a single word.
And He will not forsake us
    even though the way is steep,
For always He is near to us,
    a tender watch to keep.

And in good time He will answer us,
    and in His love He'll send
Greater things than we have asked
    and blessings without end.
So though we do not understand
    why trouble comes to man,
Can we not be contented
    just to know it is God's plan?

# When You Are Young

You are young and life is beginning
    in a wonderful way for you.
The future reaches its welcoming hand
    with new, challenging things to do.
And here is a prayer for you
    that you'll walk with God every day,
Remembering always in whatever you do
    there is only one true, righteous way.
For God in His wisdom and mercy
    looked down on His children below
And gave them the privilege of choosing
    the right or the wrong way to go.
So trust in His almighty wisdom
    and enjoy the fruit of His love,
And life on earth will be happy
    as you walk with the Father above.

# A Letter to *Mothers*

I don't know you, that is true,

And yet I almost feel I do.

Mothers' hearts are all the same

Regardless of their family name.

And I can't help but feel inside

How your heart must beam with love and pride,

For children are bright reflections, it's clear,

Of the wonderful mothers who've brought them here.

For children build their lives the way

Their mothers teach them day by day,

And all they are and all they do

They owe to mothers just like you.

And so today we honor you

For your faith helped a child to do

The right things, for you made him strong

And taught him what was right and wrong.

Without a mother's love and devotion,

No man would ever win promotion.

You taught him the fundamentals of life

And placed him then in the hands of his wife.

And together, whatever your son has won,

You can consider you both have done.

To you the credit and honor is due,

For your children's honors belong to you,

For you live in your children and what they do

Because they are a part of you.

And here is a wish that our dear God above

Will bless you today with the gift of His love.

The joy of creativity is that good feeling a person gets when he's designed or made something with his own hands. It's sad that progress sometimes means that when some things are gained, some things are also lost.

Jim Daly

# Mother's Hands

How did you learn to be a devoted, patient, and understanding mother? You knew how to solve every problem by using your talented hands, your heart, your common sense, your faith, and your trust.

*For designing and sewing costumes for recitals and plays,*
*for packing school and picnic lunches,*
*for soothing my head and holding my hand when I was ill,*
*for the standards you set and the values and virtues you taught,*

## Mother, I love you!

VJR

# IT TAKES A *Mother*

It takes a mother's love
    to make a house a home—
A place to be remembered
    no matter where we roam.
It takes a mother's patience
    to bring a child up right,

And her courage and her cheerfulness
   to make a dark day bright.
It takes a mother's thoughtfulness
   to mend the heart's deep hurts
And her skill and her endurance
   to mend little socks and shirts.
It takes a mother's kindness
   to forgive us when we err,
To sympathize in trouble
   and to bow her head in prayer.
It takes a mother's wisdom
   to recognize our needs
And to give us reassurance
   by her loving words and deeds.
It takes a mother's endless faith,
   her confidence and trust

To guide us through the pitfalls
   of selfishness and lust.
And that is why, in all this world,
   there could not be another
Who could fulfill God's purpose
   as completely as a mother.

# At My Mother's Knee

I have worshiped in churches and chapels,
    I have prayed in the busy street,
I have sought my God and found Him
    where the waves of the ocean beat.
I have knelt in a silent forest
    in the shade of an ancient tree,
But the dearest of all my altars
    was raised at my mother's knee.
God, make me the woman of her vision,
    and purge me of all selfishness,
And help keep me true to her standards,
    and help me others always to bless.
Give me grace and contentment
    whenever I face adversity,
And then keep me a pilgrim forever
    at the shrine at my mother's knee.

# DEEP IN My *Heart*

Happy little memories
      go flitting through my mind,
And in all my thoughts and memories
      I always seem to find
The picture of your face, dear,
      the memory of your touch,
And all the other little things
      I've come to love so much.
You cannot go beyond my thoughts
      or leave my love behind,
Because I keep you in my heart
      and forever on my mind.
And though I may not tell you,
      I think you know it's true
That I find daily happiness
      in the very thought of you.

# Treasured Memories

Memories grow more meaningful
    with every passing year—
More precious and more beautiful,
    more treasured and more dear.
And that is why on Mother's Day
    there comes the happy thought
Of all the treasured memories
    a mother's love has brought.

*Mothers hold their*
*children's hands for*
*the early years, but*
*their hearts forever.*
**ANCIENT SAYING**

# Understanding, Kind, and Wise

Who on earth gives more away
      and does more good for others
Than understanding, kind, and wise,
      and selfless, loving mothers,
Who ask no more than just the joy
      of helping those they love
To find in life the happiness
      that they are dreaming of.

*Of all the music that*
*reached farthest into*
*heaven, it is the beating*
*of a loving heart.*

**HENRY WARD BEECHER**

# Mother's Care

A weatherworn oak porch swing generates memories of the many moments shared with you, Mother. We would swing, talk, and plan for the "When I grow up, I want to . . ." dreams of a child. The swing was also a favorite location for offering comfort, removing splinters, and bandaging scraped knees.

*For planting the sweet peas, the morning glories, and the climbing roses,*
*for taking the time to listen to my dreams,*
*for the hours of swinging, consoling, encouraging, and planning,*

# Mother, I love you!

VJR

# Ten Little Fingers, Ten Little Toes

Ten little fingers,
    ten little toes,
Tiny as a minute,
    sweet as a rose—
One of life's mysteries,
    which nobody knows,
And one of the miracles
    only God can disclose.

*Each time a sleeping baby smiles, know that the angels are tickling it.*

**ANCIENT SAYING**

Who puts the joy in every day?

Who makes it glad in every way?

Who knows the nicest things to say?

## It's Mother

Who understands and always hears?

Who helps us dry our falling tears?

Who just grows sweeter with the years?

## It's Mother

Who is our helper and our guide?

Who always looks on us with pride?

Who's always there whate'er betide?

## It's Mother

Whom should we honor every night?

Who is a queen in her own right?

Who is her children's guiding light?

## It's Mother

# It's Mother

# WHERE THERE

Where there is love the heart is light,
Where there is love the day is bright.
Where there is love there is a song
To help when things are going wrong.
Where there is love there is a smile
To make all things seem more worthwhile.
Where there is love there's a quiet peace—
A tranquil place where turmoils cease.

# Is *Love*

Love changes darkness into light
And makes the heart take wingless flight.
And mothers have a special way
Of filling homes with love each day,
And when the home is filled with love,
You'll always find God spoken of.

# The Lingering

There's an ancient proverb that if practiced each day
Would change the whole world in a wonderful way.
Its truth is so simple, it's easy to do,
And it works every time and successfully too.
For you can't do a kindness without a reward—
Not in silver nor gold but in joy from the Lord.
You can't light a candle to show others the way
Without feeling the warmth of that bright little ray.

# Fragrance

And you can't pluck a rose all fragrant with dew

Without part of its fragrance remaining with you.

And whose hands bestow more fragrant bouquets

Than Mother, who daily speaks kind words of praise—

Mother, whose courage and comfort and cheer

Light bright little candles in hearts through the year.

No wonder the hands of an unselfish mother

Are symbols of sweetness unlike any other.

# Mother, May I Help You?

The sweet aroma of freshly washed and air-dried laundry or the sight of sheets flapping in the breeze summon up enchanting images of long ago. "Mother, may I help you?" These words so innocently asked must have been immeasurably comforting for you to hear. Your example of helping others was a lesson in living the Golden Rule. God must be pleased with the standard you set for your children to follow.

*For displaying kindness to all,*
*for being the person I hope to become,*
*for shaping me into the person I am,*

## Mother, I love you!

VJR

# Time to Be Kind

*Put on then, as God's chosen ones, holy and beloved, compassion, kindness, lowliness, meekness, and patience.*

**COLOSSIANS 3:12**

In this busy world
    it's refreshing to find
People who still have
    the time to be kind,
People still ready—
    by thought, word, or deed—
To reach out a hand
    in the hour of need,
People who still have
    the faith to believe
That the more you give
    the more you receive.

## Kindness

Kindness is a virtue
    given by the Lord—
It pays dividends in happiness
    and joy is its reward.
For if you practice kindness
    in all you say or do,
The Lord will wrap His kindness
    around your heart and you.

*Let parents
bequeath to their
children not riches,
but the spirit of
reverence.*

**PLATO**

# A Prayer for Mother

Our Father in heaven,
        whose love is divine,
Thanks for the love
        of a mother like mine.
In Thy great mercy
        look down from above
And grant this dear mother
        the gift of Your Love,
And all through the year,
        whatever betide her,
Assure her each day
        that You are beside her.
And, Father in heaven,
        show me the way
To lighten her tasks
        and brighten her day,
And bless her dear heart
        with the insight to see
That her love means more
        than the world to me.

# THANK YOU, GOD, FOR Little THINGS

Thank you, God, for little things
    that often come our way—
The things we take for granted
    and don't mention when we pray—
The unexpected courtesy,
    the thoughtful, kindly deed,
A hand reached out to help us
    in the time of sudden need.
Oh, make us more aware, dear God,
    of little daily graces
That come to us with sweet surprise
    from never-dreamed-of places.

69

# Heart Gifts

It's not the things that can be bought

      that are life's richest treasures—

It's just the little "heart gifts"

      that money cannot measure.

A cheerful smile, a friendly word,

      a sympathetic nod

Are priceless little treasures

      from the storehouse of our God.

They are the things that can't be bought
with silver or with gold,
For thoughtfulness and kindness
and love are never sold.
They are the priceless things in life
for which no one can pay,
And the giver finds rich recompense
in giving them away.

# Mother and Family

"This little piggy went to market. This little piggy stayed home . . ."
The front porch was the perfect setting for nursery rhymes, games of
checkers, husking corn, and shelling peas. The porch of yesterday was
the family room of today. Families gathered there and shared the good
times and the bad.

*For the ice cold lemonade you served on warm summer afternoons,*
*for making time to listen to my concerns,*
*for disciplining with love,*
*for praying and encouraging spiritual growth,*

## Mother, I love you!

VJR

# MOTHER'S CARE

You mother every living thing
From poodle dogs to birds that sing.
You give a mother's tender care
To marigolds and maidenhair.
You gently nurture tiny seeds
And help fulfill their growing needs.
You pet and pamper pet tomatoes
And fondle onions and potatoes.
All growing things get your attention
And much, much more than I can mention.
You lend your many loving ways
And spread your sunny little rays
Among God's creatures everywhere
And give them all a mother's care.
So on today I salute all mothers,
Because of their care for others.

# Peace Begins in the Home

Peace is not something you fight for
> with bombs and missiles that kill,

Nor can it be won in a battle of words
> man fashions by scheming and skill.

For men who are greedy and warlike,
> whose avarice for power cannot cease,

Can never contribute in helping
> to bring this world nearer to peace.

For in seeking peace for all people,
> there is only one place to begin,

And that is within each home and heart,
> for the fortress of peace is within.

*There is beauty all around when there's peace at home.*

**AUTHOR UNKNOWN**

# A Perfect
## Time

Mother's Day is a perfect time
for compliments and praise
And saying all the nice things
we don't say other days,
A time for reminiscing
and looking back with pleasure
On happy little incidents
the heart has come to treasure.

*Home is the one place in all
this world where hearts are
sure of each other. It is the
place of confidence.*

**FREDERICK W. ROBERTSON**

May the knowledge that your children
and their sweet children too
Care for you and love you
just because you're you
Keep you ever happy
when lonely hours appear,
Knowing that their love for you
is all around you, dear.

# Their Love Is All around You

*There is an enduring tenderness*
*in the love of a mother.*

**WASHINGTON IRVING**

*From
A to Z
a mother
is an . . .*

ADMINISTRATOR

BAKER

COUNSELOR

DIPLOMAT

EFFICIENCY EXPERT

FRIEND

GARDENER

HOME ECONOMIST

INSPIRATIONALIST

JUDGE

KITCHEN AUTHORITY

LEADER

MEDIATOR

NURTURER

ORGANIZER

PEDAGOGUE

QUALITY ANALYST

RECREATION LEADER

SPIRITUAL DIRECTOR

TEACHER

UMPIRE

VACATION PLANNER

WILLING WORKER

X-MAS AND HOLIDAY ACTIVITIES DIRECTOR

YOUTH PLAYGROUND SUPERVISOR

ZEST-FILLED ENCOURAGER

*The hand that rocks the cradle rules the world.*

**W. R. WALLACE**

VJR